KING*f*ISHER

First
Thesaurus

GEORGE BEAL

Illustrated by Martin Chatterton

Consulting Editor: Jayne Hyman, B. S., M. Ed.

KING*f*ISHER

NEW YORK

KINGFISHER
Larousse Kingfisher Chambers Inc.
80 Maiden Lane
New York, New York 10038

First published in hardcover in 1993
First published in paperback in 2001
10 9 8 7 6 5 4 3 (HC)
10 9 8 7 6 5 4 3 2 1 (PB)
PB - 1TR / 0501 / DUR / 140MSTR

LIBRARY OF CONGRESS CATALOGING-IN-PUBLICATION DATA
Beal, George.
    The Kingfisher first thesaurus / George Beal :
[illustrations by] Martin Chatterton. —1st American ed.
    p.   cm.
    Summary: An illustrated thesaurus containing over 100 keywords
accompanied by their synonyms, antonyms, and homonyms. Also
includes example sentences to explain shades of meaning and games
to play with words.
    1. English language—Synonyms and antonyms—Juvenile literature.
[1. English language—Synonyms and antonyms.] I. Chatterton,
Martin, ill. II. Title.
PE1591.B38   1993
423'.1—dc20 92-45572 CIP AC

ISBN 1-85697-914-8 (HC)
ISBN 0-7534-5409-2 (PB)

Printed in Hungary

Consulting editor: Jane Hyman, B. S. Boston University
(Elementary Education); M. Ed. Boston University (Reading);
M. Ed. Tufts University (Special Needs); Ed. D. (Candidate:
Administration and Supervision); Principal, M. L. Donovan
Elementary School, Randolph, Massachusetts.

Editor: John Grisewood
Coordinating editor: Debra Miller
Design concept: Steve Leaning
Designer: Robert Wheeler

Introduction

The word *thesaurus* is from the Greek for "treasury," and that, indeed, is what it is — a rich treasury of words from which you can pick and choose at will.

In this thesaurus we have selected over a hundred commonly used words and listed with them other words with similar meanings (the technical word for another word with a similar meaning is *synonym*). If you look up *pick*, for instance, you will be given four other words: *choose, gather, pluck,* and *select*. Wouldn't it be much easier, you may ask, if we had only one word for each idea or object? Take the word *nice*, for example, a commonly overused word:

After their *nice* supper, the kittens went to sleep on a *nice* cushion. It was then that I considered how *nice* it was of that *nice* woman next door to offer to look after them while we are away having a *nice* time. We must buy her a *nice* present, maybe a *nice* straw hat so that she can have a *nice* time sitting in the sun in her *nice* garden.

All those *nices* make this passage sound flat and repetitious. Here is an alternative version:

After their *delicious* supper, the kittens went to sleep on a *comfortable* cushion. It was then that I considered how *thoughtful* it was of that *kind* woman next door to offer to look after them while we are away having an *enjoyable* time. We must buy her a *special* present, maybe a *pretty* straw hat so that she can have a *pleasant* time sitting in the sun in her *lovely* garden.

You can see from this passage that it is worth looking for the exact word to give life to what you are trying to say.

It is important to remember that the lists of words under each keyword in this book are words of similar meaning, for there are few words which mean exactly the same as another. Take the word *fast* for instance. It means almost the same as *quick*, yet we would speak of a *fast car* or a *fast train* but not of a *quick car* or a *quick train*. So you must use synonyms with care. That is why there are sample sentences to show how to use the word correctly.

A thesaurus is a fascinating word-finder, a source book, a priceless treasury which shows the marvelous variety and richness of the English language. English, more than any other language, has borrowed words from all around the world and absorbed and anglicized them. Onto the plain and simple language of the Anglo-Saxons has been added a vast hoard of Latin and Norman French words — so that the Old English *forgive, gift*, and *give* are matched by *pardon, present,* and *donate* from Latin and Norman French. Thousands of words stem from Greek, the language of learning. Where would we be without *electronics, phones, oxygen,* and *electricity*? From the Germans we get *dachshunds, hamburgers,* and *kindergartens*. To Turkey we owe *divans, kiosks, tulips,* and *yogurt*. To Spain we are grateful for *siestas, canteens,* and *guerillas*. The Arabs provide us with *cotton, syrup, sofas,* and *mattresses*, the Dutch with *brandy, landscapes, sleighs, wagons,* and *yachts*. And so on, around the world.

We hope you derive hours of pleasure from browsing through your thesaurus, and that you will discover the joy and satisfaction of writing a letter or story that conveys what you want to say, exactly and in an interesting way.

How to use your thesaurus

All the entry words that appear in this thesaurus are in alphabetical order, for example: *bar, barbecue, bashful, battle, bear, beat,* and so on. All words that are not keywords tell you to look up another word, which is usually a keyword and sometimes the opposite of a keyword. If you look up *acquaintance* it will say *see friend*; *arrive* will tell you to look up *come* and *the opposite of leave*.

When you reach one of the keywords, an arrow points to a panel, which is usually illustrated. The panel contains other words with similar meanings. So under *beautiful* are its synonyms: *fair, handsome, lovely,* and *pretty*.

The keyword *beautiful* is followed by its part of speech in italic type (*adjective*).

The word is then defined as it would be in a dictionary: *Something we enjoy looking at, or someone who is very good-looking or attractive, is described as beautiful.* This is followed by at least one example of how the word *beautiful* can be used.

Each synonym in the list below the keyword is followed by a sample sentence. Sometimes there is a further list of synonyms, but without sample sentences. For example, under *beautiful* you will find *cute, gorgeous, splendid,* and *sweet*. These are headed, "Other words."

Where they exist, the opposite words (antonyms) are given. If the opposite word is also a keyword, it says simply, "see such and such a word." If the opposite word is not a keyword, a sample sentence is included.

Where there is a word with the same sound as the keyword (a homonym) we include it with a sample sentence. For example, under *break* the "Same sound" word is *brake*, followed by a sentence.

Topic pages

An important part of this thesaurus are the special, highly illustrated, topic features. The topics range from animals, houses, and music, to sports, travel, and weather. These pages contain such things as different word groups — *river, brook, stream; guitar, violin, cello* — as well as word games, palindromes (look that up in a dictionary!), homonyms, rhymes, and limericks. They are intended to help you extend your vocabulary and to add a little fun.

A

abandon
see leave

able

able *(adjective)*

You are **able** to do something if you are good at it, or are well enough to do it: *If I go to France, I will be able to speak French, because I learned it at school.*

adept   Jo is so **adept** with her pocketknife, she has carved a pattern on that stick.

capable   Our teacher is **capable** of making us laugh; she's very funny.

skillful   My mother is **skillful** — a brilliant artist and a wonderful teacher.

strong   Elephants are **strong** enough to lift whole tree trunks.

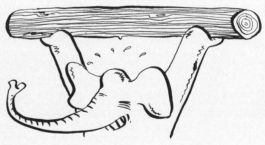

talented   What a **talented** family! Steve plays the violin, and Mary plays the piano.

Opposite word

unskilled   The table fell apart because it was made by **unskilled** workers.

about →

ache *see* hurt

acquaintance *see* friend

adept *see* able

adjust *see* change

admirable *see* good

admire *see* like

adore *see* love

affect *see* touch

affection *see* love

afraid →

aged *see* old

aid *see* help

aim *see* try

about *(adverb)*

When you use the word **about**, it is usually because you are not certain exactly: *It's **about** time we started. We went to Bermuda **about** six months ago.*

almost	It's **almost** twelve o'clock; we must hurry to catch the train.
nearly	This piece of cloth is **nearly** the right length.
around	*(preposition)* Wherever we went, there were flowers all **around** us.

afraid *(adjective)*

When you think something nasty may happen or if you are full of fear, you can often use the word **afraid**: *When I was very little, I was **afraid** of the dark.*

frightened	Who's **frightened** of ghosts?
nervous	Henry was **nervous** about going to the dentist.
scared	Don't be **scared**; the bull only looks fierce.

Opposite words *see* bold

airy
  see light

alarm
  see fright

almost
  see about

alone
  see lonely

alter
  see change

amusing
  see funny

ancient
  see old

angry

answer
  see opposite
  of ask

antique
  see old

appear
  see come

approach
  see come

angry *(adjective)*

If someone annoys you or is rude to you, you are likely to be **angry**: *The teacher was angry when Susan forgot her report.*

cross Mark was **cross** when Anne won.

furious Dan is **furious** when I'm late.

indignant Sarah was **indignant** when Pete accused her of telling lies.

irate The **irate** driver shook her fist at the car in front of her when it stopped without warning.

mad My mother was **mad** at me when I smashed the window.

upset Jill was **upset** when Adam rode his bike over her foot.

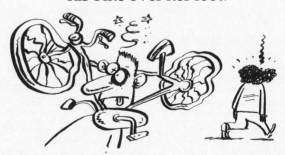

Other words annoyed, irritable, worked up

Opposite words

friendly Keith gave me a **friendly** smile.

pleased I was **pleased** with the photo.

All about animals

Birds fly

Animal movements

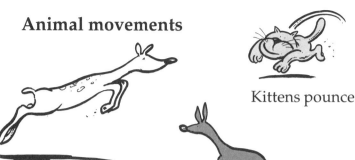

Kittens pounce

Frogs hop

Deer leap

Kangaroos bound

Cheetahs run

Fish swim

Caterpillars creep

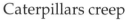

Kinds of animal

Mammals give birth to live young which they suckle with milk. They include humans, dogs, elephants, kangaroos (known as marsupials), and sea mammals such as whales and dolphins.

Amphibians are animals such as frogs, toads, and newts. Most start their lives in water.

Reptiles include snakes, lizards, tortoises, and crocodiles. In prehistoric times reptiles ruled the Earth.

Birds developed from reptiles. All birds lay eggs. Some birds, such as the kiwi, cannot fly.

Insects are the most numerous of all the different kinds of animal. They live all over the world.

Spiders Unlike insects, spiders have eight legs. All spiders spin silk threads.

Fish were the first animals with backbones (vertebrates) to develop on Earth. Fish breathe through gills.

Animal terms

animal	group	male	female	young
donkey	herd	jackass	jenny	foal
cat	litter	tom	queen	kitten
cattle	herd	bull	cow	calf
dog	pack	dog	bitch	pup
fox	skulk	dog	vixen	cub
goat	herd	billy	nanny	kid
goose	flock	goose	gander	gosling
horse	herd	stallion	mare	foal
				filly (female)
				colt (male)
lion	pride	lion	lioness	cub
pig	herd	boar	sow	piglet
seal	colony	bull	cow	pup
sheep	flock	ram	ewe	lamb
whale	school	bull	cow	calf

Animal homes

Tigers live in the jungle.

Hippopotamuses live in rivers.

Frogs live in ponds.

Bats live in caves.

Camels live in deserts.

Whales live in the sea.

Animal sounds

Bees *buzz*

Cats *meow*

Cockerels *crow*

Cows *moo*

Crows *caw*

Dogs *bark*

Ducks *quack*

Horses *neigh*

Lions *roar*

Mice *squeak*

Owls *hoot*

Pigs *grunt*

Snakes *hiss*

Wolves *howl*

arid
see dry *and*
opposite of wet

around
see about

arrest
see catch

arrive
see come *and*
opposite of leave

ascend
see rise

ask

assist
see help

attempt
see try

average
see fair

awful
see hard

ask *(verb)*

To **ask**, you speak in order to get information about something: *If you want to find out about stamps, then **ask** a stamp collector.*

beg The defendant **begged** for mercy.

demand *To order or require:*
I **demand** more money.

inquire *To ask questions:*
May I inquire what time it is?

invite *To ask someone to do something:*
Ian **invited** me to his party.

query "Are you sure how to spell *inoculate*?" the teacher **queried**.

request She **requested** us to stand up.

Opposite word

answer Will you **answer** my questions?

B

bad

bake
see cook

bar
see shut

barbecue
see cook

bashful
*see opposite
of* bold

battle
see fight

bad *(adjective)*

When something is not good, or is wrong or harmful, we say that it is **bad**: *Sue's writing is so **bad**, I find it hard to read. They say that we shall have **bad** weather tomorrow.*

dangerous   This road is not safe; there are many **dangerous** corners.

disagreeable   We didn't enjoy the party; the guests were so **disagreeable**.

evil   Demons, ghouls, and goblins are all **evil** spirits.

nasty   My mother scolded me for being **nasty** to my brother.

naughty   *Ill-behaved or disobedient*: Michael was very **naughty**; he pulled the cat's tail.

rotten   *Spoiled, or poor in quality*: All the fruit was **rotten**.

sour   We couldn't use the milk as it had gone **sour**.

Other words harmful, horrible, horrid, mischievous, repulsive, vile, wicked

Opposite words *see* good

bear
 see take

beat
 see hit

beautiful

become
 see get, grow

beg
 see ask

begin
 see start

believe
 see think

bend
 see turn

bestow
 see give

beautiful *(adjective)*

Something we enjoy looking at, or someone who is very good-looking or attractive, is described as **beautiful**: *My mother is wearing a **beautiful** dress. It was such a **beautiful** day that we went to the beach.*

fair Cinderella was **fairer** than her stepsisters.

handsome The black horse was a truly **handsome** creature.

lovely These flowers are **lovely**.

pretty I think pink is a **pretty** color.

Other words cute, gorgeous, splendid, sweet

Opposite word

ugly Some deep-sea fish look really **ugly**.

big

bit
see piece

blank
see empty

blend
see mix

blond(e)
see fair

big *(adjective)*

Something is called **big** because it is sizable or important: *Canada is a very **big** country, although it does not have a large population.*

enormous	Jumbo jets are **enormous**.
great	*Famous or prominent:* Babe Ruth was one of America's **great** baseball players.
heavy	In the old days **heavy**, unwieldy steam engines pulled trains.
huge	The giant has **huge** muscles.
large	Paris and Rio are **large** cities.
vast	The desert is too **vast** to cross.
wide	The **wide** truck can't get down this narrow street.

Other words adult, colossal, gigantic

Opposite words

little	There was **little** hope of finding the missing aircraft.
small	That hole is so **small**, only a mouse could get through.
tiny	Ants have **tiny** legs.

13

blunt
  see dull

boil
  see cook

boisterous
  see loud, rough

bold

bolt
  see escape

boring
  see dull

boundary
  see end

brainy
  see clever

brave
  see bold

brawny
  see strong

bold *(adjective)*

Bold people face danger without fear: *The early explorers were* **bold**, *unafraid of the unknown.*

brave	The **brave** firefighters ran up a ladder to the window.
courageous	Sharon was **courageous** in rescuing the cat from the tree.

daring	Martha was **daring** enough to climb the steeple.

Other words adventurous, heroic, rude

Same sound

bowled	I **bowled** a perfect game.

Opposite words

bashful	Susan is so **bashful**; she never speaks until spoken to.
shy	Chris is **shy** with new people.
timid	*Lacking in confidence*: Jo's too **timid** to pat the horse.

break

bright
see clear

bring
see get, take

build
see make

bulging
see full

bump
see hit

buoyant
see light

bury
see hide

break *(verb)*

When you **break** something, it comes apart, falls to pieces, or stops working: *Be careful you don't **break** the eggs!*

crack	Don't **crack** nuts with your teeth!
fracture	*If we break a bone, we fracture it*: Al **fractured** his arm in the gym.
shatter	*To break into tiny pieces*: The ball hit the window, and the glass **shattered**.
smash	*To hit something, making it break*: I **smashed** two cups and saucers.
split	Sue **split** the logs in two.

Same sound

brake	The car **braked** at the corner.

Opposite words

fix	*To put together, or repair*: Sue **fixed** the broken plate with glue.
mend	I must **mend** my torn jacket.
repair	I'll soon **repair** this old clock.

C

call *(verb)*

We **call** when we cry out, either for help or simply to attract attention, or when we telephone someone. *Will you* ***call*** *me when dinner's ready?* ***Call*** *me and we'll make a date.*

cry   My little brother started to **cry** when Dad went to work.

name   I **named** my cat "Fluffy."

shout   "Of course I can control my dog!" she **shouted**.

visit   I'll **visit** my relatives when I go home.

yell   Our team scored first, and the fans **yelled** with delight.

calm *(adjective)*

It is **calm** when things are quiet and untroubled: *After the terrible storm, the wind dropped and all was **calm** once more.*

peaceful   At night the woods are very noisy, not at all **peaceful**!

placid   Joe's an excitable man, but his wife is quiet and **placid**.

still   He lay very **still** in the long grass, watching the lions.

see also quiet

Opposite words

disturbed   I had a **disturbed** night's sleep; my neighbors had a party.

stormy   We can't go skydiving in this **stormy** weather.

capable
  see able

capture
  see catch, take

careful

careful *(adjective)*

If we take care and pay attention to what we are doing, we are **careful**: *My grandfather is a careful driver, always aware of other drivers.*

cautious	Be **cautious** on that mountain; there are some steep slopes.

wary	The deer were **wary** of the approaching hunters.
watchful	We were **watchful** as the boat neared the rocky shore.

Opposite words

careless	Tina's work is **careless**; she needs to try harder.
forgetful	Jim's so **forgetful**; he thought it was Wednesday.
rash	Annie is so **rash**; she never thinks what might happen!
thoughtless	Bill has left the door open; he's so **thoughtless**.

careless
see opposite
of careful

carry
see take

catch

catch *(verb)*

When we **catch** something, we stop it and get hold of it: *We went out in a boat to **catch** fish.*

arrest   Two police officers **arrested** the thief.

capture   After the lion escaped, it took three hours to **capture** it.

grab   Tim **grabbed** the toy and made his brother cry.

Other words grasp, snatch

Opposite word

release   The war was over, and it was time to **release** all prisoners.

miss   The catcher **missed** the ball.

cautious
  see careful

certain
  see sure

change

chat
  see talk

cheerful
  see happy *and*
  opposite of sad

chew
  see eat

change *(verb)*

You **change** something if you make it differ- ent or put something in its place: *I'll change my clothes before dinner.*

adjust	You can **adjust** the height of the chair.
alter	I'll **alter** the room by replacing the wallpaper.
exchange	I had a yellow hat but I **exchanged** it for a blue one.
modify	The car cost too much to make, so they had to **modify** it.
swap	I collect Australian stamps and **swap** Canadian ones for them.
vary	Dogs **vary** in size from Irish wolfhounds to Chihuahuas.

see also turn

Other words amend, convert, replace, revise, transform

Opposite words

conserve	We've **conserved** the house's Colonial-style exterior.
retain	Rita **retains** her old name.

chilly
  see cold

choose
  see pick

chop
  see cut

chuckle
  see laugh

clamor
  see noise

clean
  *see opposite
  of* dirty

clear

clear *(adjective)*

If something is easy to see through, or without obstacles, we say it is **clear**: *It was a lovely day; the sky was **clear** and cloudless. The answer to the problem is **clear**.*

bright   A **bright** beam shone on the car.

obvious   *Plain to see:*
We're lost; it's **obvious** we've taken the wrong turn.

plain   It's **plain** you've got mumps.

pure   The glass contained **pure** water.

simple   There is no **simple** answer to such a complicated question.

see also empty, plain

Opposite words

dim   The lights on my bike are **dim** because the battery is low.

misty   It's too **misty** to see the tower.

see also dull

clever

clip
  see cut

close
  see shut

closed
  see shut

clutch
  see hold

clutter
  see mess

clever *(adjective)*

People who are **clever** are sharp-witted and have a quick mind: *Debbie is really **clever**; she'll probably become a professor at least!*

brainy   Isaac was so **brainy**, he could count when he was three!

cunning   Foxes are **cunning** and sly.

intelligent My dog is very **intelligent**; she can do 20 different tricks.

talented   Yehudi Menuhin was a **talented** boy. He could play the violin in concerts when he was seven.

see also able

Opposite words

stupid   Our parrot can't speak a single word; she's too **stupid**!

see also dull

coarse
see rough

cold

collect
see get

combat
see fight

combine
see mix

cold *(adjective)*

When the temperature gets low, we say it is **cold**: *The weather in Siberia is very **cold**.*

chilly   I need more blankets on my bed; the room was **chilly** last night.

cool   After the heat of summer, it's nice to have a few **cool** breezes.

freezing   The water on the pond is **freezing**. Let's go skating.

Other words crisp, frosty, icy, nippy

Opposite word

hot   The sun had heated the sand, making it too **hot** to sit on.

The community's helping hands

Teachers and professors help us to learn.

Doctors make sick people better.

Firefighters put out fires and rescue people.

Mailwomen and mailmen deliver our mail.

Garbage collectors take away our garbage.

Dentists look after our teeth.

Other words for teacher
coach   educator   schoolmaster   schoolmistress
instructor   lecturer   professor   trainer   tutor

Ambulance drivers take the sick and injured to hospital.

Priests and rabbis advise and console people.

Nurses look after the sick.

Cooks prepare meals.

The police help keep us safe.

Bus drivers take us to school and work.

Match the people above with these places:
church   synagogue   fire station   hospital   school
post office   kitchen   police station

come

comfortable
see nice

comical
see funny

commence
see start

companion
see friend

compel
see make

complete
see full

complicated
see hard *and*
opposite of plain

comrade
see friend

conceal
see hide

conclude
see end, think

confident
see sure

come *(verb)*

If you move toward someone, they will say that you have **come**: *Uncle Bill has just come back from South America.*

appear	I went out to meet Jenny, and she **appeared** at the end of the street.
approach	A police officer **approached** our car to warn us of an accident.
arrive	Guests started to **arrive** at six o'clock.
enter	When you reach the theater, **enter** by the stage door.
happen	Hanukkah **happens** once a year.
occur	The Sabbath **occurs** every week.

Opposite words *see* go, leave

connect
see join

conserve
*see opposite
of* change

consider
see think

console
*see opposite
of* hurt

construct
see make

contain
see hold

contented
see happy

continue
see go, keep

convey
see send

cook

cool
see cold

correct
see right *and
opposite of* wrong

courageous
see bold

cover
see hide

cook *(verb)*

If you **cook** food, you heat it in some way to prepare it for eating: *My father taught me how to **cook**, and my brother learned, too!*

bake   You **bake** cakes in an oven.

barbecue   In the summer we **barbecue** food on a fire outside.

boil   **Boil** some water for tea.

fry   We **fried** bacon for breakfast.

grill   You **grill** tomatoes without oil.

roast   We **roasted** chestnuts in the fire.

stew   All the apples were put into a pot, and then we **stewed** them.

toast   We **toasted** marshmallows on the fire.

Containers

glass   cup   mug   tumbler   goblet

box   crate   chest   safe   can

envelope

pocket

Double words

Fill in the missing word in the center of each line, remembering that the clues on each side refer to it.

pot _ _ _ _ _ _ ship

tin _ _ _ able

bag _ _ _ _ dismiss

basin _ _ _ _ submerge

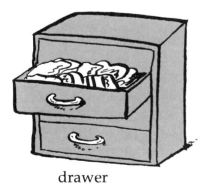

vase

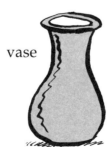

aquarium

drawer

bucket

baggage

suitcase

trunk

pitcher

jar

sack

bag

pack

bowl

cone

briefcase

knapsack

sink
basin

flowerpot

basket

wheelbarrow

saucepan

casserole

tray

frying pan

skillet

crack
  see break

cross
  see angry

crude
  see rough

cry
  see call *and*
  opposite of laugh

cunning
  see clever

cut

cut *(verb)*

If you **cut** something, you divide it by using something sharp: *Ben took the scissors and **cut** the card into three pieces.*

chop   Margaret **chopped** the logs into firewood with her new ax.

clip   Who'll **clip** the hedge?

prune   Now's the time to **prune** the roses.

saw   I'll **saw** these planks in no time with my new electric saw.

slice   If you **slice** the bread, I'll make the sandwiches.

snip   I don't need all that parsley. Can you **snip** a little off the bunch?

trim   The barber **trimmed** my hair.

D

damage
see hurt

damp
see wet

dangerous
see bad

daring
see bold

dash
see hurry, run

dawdle
see opposite
of hurry

declare
see say

decline
see opposite
of rise

decrease
see opposite of
grow, rise

delay
see opposite
of hurry

delicate
see soft, weak,
and opposite of
rough

delicious
see nice

delighted
see happy

demand
see ask

demonstrate
see show

dense
see opposite
of thin

deny
see opposite
of give

depart
see go, leave

deposit
see put

depressed
see sad

descend
see fall *and*
opposite of rise

desert
see leave

destroy
see opposite
of make

develop
see grow

devour
see eat

difficult
see hard

difficulty
see mess

dim
see opposite
of clear

din
see noise

dine
see eat

dirty

disagreeable
  see bad

discard
  see opposite
  of keep

disconnect
  see opposite
  of join

discover
  see find

discuss
  see talk

disguise
  see hide

dismal
  see sad

dismay
  see fright

dispatch
  see send

display
  see show

distrustful
  see opposite
  of sure

dirty *(adjective)*

If something is not clean, we say that it's **dirty**: *We took our **dirty** towels to the laundromat.*

filthy   His glasses are so **filthy**, he can hardly see through them.

foul   The ship's cargo had gone bad, and there was a **foul** smell.

grimy   A hundred years ago, **grimy** urchins begged in the streets.

impure   This water is **impure**. You'll be ill if you drink it.

polluted   The atmosphere is **polluted** with car fumes.

soiled   Her shoes were **soiled** with mud.

Other words shabby, stained, unclean

Opposite word

clean   Do you have a **clean** shirt?

disturbed
see opposite
of calm

disturbing
see opposite
of quiet

donate
see give

doubtful
see opposite
of sure

drab
see dull

drag
see pull

draw
see pull

drawing
see picture

drop
see fall

dry

dry *(adjective)*

When anything is without moisture or wetness, we say that it is **dry**: *We've had such a dry summer, there will be a poor harvest.*

arid   Parched, **arid** land is caused by drought.

parched   What a hot day! I'm thirsty and my throat is **parched**.

uninteresting   Mark reads such dry books; they look so **uninteresting**.

Other words boring, monotonous, tedious

Opposite words *see* wet

dull *(adjective)*

If something is not very bright or interesting, we can say that it is **dull**: *We switched off the TV because the programs were so **dull**.*

blunt   My pencil point is **blunt**; can you lend me your sharpener?

boring   They spent the evening playing cards, which I think is **boring**.

drab   When it rains, the **drab** streets look even more miserable.

gloomy   The paper was full of **gloomy** news of wars and disasters.

Other words misty, monotonous, tedious

Opposite words

sharp   That ax won't cut unless it's **sharp**.

see also bright, clear, clever, interesting

E

earn
  see get, make

eat

eat *(verb)*

When we **eat**, we take food into our bodies: *I like to **eat** ice cream in the summer.*

chew   Our new puppy has just **chewed** my slippers.

devour   Caterpillars have **devoured** the cabbages.

dine   We **dined** at the new Chinese restaurant.

gorge   Nick had a stomachache after he **gorged** on all the apples.

nibble   Rabbits **nibble** carrots.

swallow   Harry **swallowed** a fishbone, and it stuck in his throat.

effort
  see try, work

employment
  see work

empty

empty *(adjective)*

If something, such as a box, has nothing in it, we say it is **empty**: *Amy drank the milk until the glass was empty.*

blank   Here's a **blank** sheet of paper.

clear   Sweep the path until it's **clear**.

unoccupied We rang the bell, but the house was **unoccupied**.

vacant   We couldn't stay at the hotel; they had no **vacant** rooms.

void   *(noun)* The planet was uninhabited; it was just a **void**.

see also clear

Opposite words

occupied   The phone booth was **occupied**, so we had to wait.

packed   The room was **packed** with people.

see also full

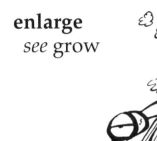

end

enemy
see opposite
of friend

enjoyable
see nice

enlarge
see grow

enormous
see big

enter
see come

entertaining
see interesting

entire
see full

end (verb)

This can be either a *verb*: *We shall* **end** *our meeting this afternoon.* Or it can be a *noun*: *We reached the* **end** *of our journey feeling tired.*

conclude	The teachers **concluded** their talk after an hour.
finish	The game **finished** at four o'clock.
terminate	The train **terminates** here, but you can take a bus to the town.
boundary	(*noun*) The Rhine River marks the **boundary** between several countries.

Opposite words *see* start

escape *(verb)*

When you **escape**, you get away, get free, or get out: *The prisoner's door was locked, but he managed to escape through the window.*

bolt   The horse **bolted** out of the stable.

flee   The thief **fled** from the police.

Opposite words *see* catch

F

faint
see weak

fair

fair *(adjective)*

If you are honest and play by the rules, you can be called **fair**: *Mrs. Jones is always fair, and has no favorites.* **Fair** also means having light-colored hair or skin.

average	It wasn't a great movie, only **average**.
blond(e)	My son has wonderful **blond** hair.
just	My father is stern, but **just**.
light	He was pale, with **light** skin.
mediocre	This is a **mediocre** report; it's really not very good.
reasonable	These prices are **reasonable**.

see also beautiful, light

Same sound

fare	*(noun)* How much is the bus **fare** to the zoo?

Opposite words

fraudulent	It was a **fraudulent** business, selling brass rings as gold ones.
unfair	The referee was **unfair**, and favored the home team.

fall

fall *(verb)*

Something **falls** if it drops down or becomes lower: *These stairs are so steep, I'm afraid I might fall.*

descend   The elevator **descended** from the third floor to the first floor.

drop   **Drop** a coin in the fountain and make a wish.

sink   Soon that submarine will **sink** below the surface.

trip   He **tripped** over a stone.

tumble   Jill **tumbled** down the hill.

Opposite words *see* rise

false
 see wrong *and*
 opposite of right

famous
 see important

fascinating
 see interesting

fast

fast *(adjective)*

Something that moves at speed can be called **fast**: *We caught a **fast** train and were soon home.* **Fast** can also mean fixed and steady.

firm	She stood there, **firm** as a rock.
quick	I know a **quick** way to the town.
rapid	We crossed the river with a few **rapid** strokes of the oars.
secure	The boat is tied up and **secure**.
swift	It was a **swift** river, with a strong current.

Opposite words

gradual	There has been a **gradual** change in the weather.
slow	Our new car is a bit **slow**.

Family

Everyone is part of a family. If people marry they become part of a new family.

parent
mother
father
son
daughter
brother
sister
husband
wife
child
children

uncle
aunt
cousin
nephew
niece

mother-in-law
father-in-law
son-in-law
daughter-in-law

stepmother
stepfather
foster-mother
foster-father
stepson
stepdaughter

grandmother
grandfather
grandson
granddaughter

great-grandmother
great-grandfather
great-grandson
great-granddaughter
great-uncle
great-aunt
great-niece
great-nephew

A man and a woman were at a party. The man pointed to a boy across the room and said, "That's my nephew." His sister said, "That's not my nephew." Can you figure this out?

Family problems

What relation is . . .

Mr. Bowles to his
son's daughter?

Mrs. Jones to her
sister's brother?

John to his
mother's husband?

Deri to her uncle's son?

Who is your Dad's father?

Monday's child is fair of face,
Tuesday's child is full of grace,
Wednesday's child is full of woe,
Thursday's child has far to go,
Friday's child is loving and giving,
Saturday's child works hard for a living,
And the child that is born on the Sabbath day
Is bonny and blithe, and good and gay.

Solomon Grundy,

Born on Monday,

Christened on Tuesday,

Married on Wednesday,

Took ill on Thursday,

Worse on Friday,

Died on Saturday,

Buried on Sunday,

This is the end

of Solomon Grundy.

43

fasten
  see join, shut

fear
  see fright

feeble
  see weak

feel

feel *(verb)*

If you come into contact with something, or get an impression of something, you **feel** it: *This cloth **feels** like silk; it's so smooth.*

experience You'll **experience** a sense of achievement when you have learned to swim.

handle **Handle** the china with great care.

sense Sue **sensed** that something was wrong.

suffer If you have a toothache, you will **suffer** some pain.

touch If I reach up high enough, I can **touch** the ceiling.

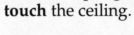

see also touch

fetch
  see get

few
  *see opposite
  of* many

fight

fight (*verb*)

When you **fight**, you try to hurt somebody, or you make an effort to do something: *I had to **fight** to get people to listen to my story.*

battle   The wrestlers **battled** for the world championship.

combat   Judge Smith will always **combat** every form of injustice.

oppose   The local people **opposed** the plan for a new service station.

quarrel   I'm sorry Naomi and I **quarreled**; she's my best friend.

struggle   Jack **struggled** to knot his tie.

Opposite words

reconcile   My two brothers had argued for years, but are now **reconciled**.

filthy
  see dirty

find

fine
  see good, thin

finger
  see touch

finish
  see end

firm
  see fast, hard,
  strong, sure

fit
  see good

fix
  *see opposite
  of* break

flat
  see smooth

flee
  see escape

flimsy
  see light, weak

find *(verb)*

If you unearth something, or come across it unexpectedly, you **find** it: *Let's go to the beach and see if we can **find** some seashells.*

discover We **discovered** a mistake in the book.

locate Can you **locate** your home town on the map?

trace The police were unable to **trace** the missing painting.

work out Can you **work out** the answer?

Opposite word

lose I would hate to **lose** my watch.

see also opposite of hide

float
  see rise

flow
  see run

fluffy
  see soft

flutter
  see shake

foe
  *see opposite
  of* friend

force
  see push

forgetful
  *see opposite
  of* careful

form
  see make

forsake
  see leave
  and opposite
  of keep

foul
  see dirty

fracture
  see break

fragment
  see piece

frail
  see weak

frank
  see plain

fraudulent
  see opposite
  of fair

freezing
  see cold

frequent
  see many

friend →

friend *(noun)*

Anyone whom you know well and like, can be called a **friend**: *Friends like doing things together.*

acquaintance I don't know him well; he's more of an **acquaintance** than a friend.

companion She was my **companion** at school and when we worked in an office.

comrade Andy was my **comrade** when we were in the army together.

pal Meet Jeff, an old **pal** of mine.

Opposite words

enemy Moriarty was a deadly **enemy** of Sherlock Holmes.

foe Who goes there? Friend or **foe**?

friendless
  see lonely

friendly
  see good *and*
  opposite of angry

fright

fright *(noun)*

When you feel afraid or fearful, you are
experiencing **fright**: *I had a terrible* **fright** *when
I thought I saw a ghost.*

alarm   Shouts of **alarm** arose as the
              soldiers entered the town.

dismay   We looked with **dismay** at the
              wreckage left by the storm.

fear   The antelope's eyes were wide
              with **fear** as the lion sprang.

panic   The floodwaters swirled into the
              town, spreading **panic**.

terror   The greatest **terror** of the jungle
              is fire.

frightened
see afraid

fry
see cook

full

full *(adjective)*

If something is **full**, there is no space for anything more: *We couldn't get seats for the theater because it was **full**.*

complete   Jennifer has a **complete** set of stamps for the Olympic Games.

entire   I received a class prize in front of the **entire** school.

bulging   Santa carried a **bulging** sackful of presents.

packed   The attic is **packed** with junk.

Other words crammed, filled, jammed, overflowing

Opposite words *see* empty

funny

furious
  see angry

funny *(adjective)*

Anything that makes you laugh or that is unusual or surprising, can be called **funny**: *There were many funny people in the movies, but the best was Charlie Chaplin.*

amusing   The children like Clare; she's such an **amusing** talker.

comical   With her battered hat and false nose, she was a **comical** clown.

humorous   The audience roared with laughter at the comedian's **humorous** stories.

odd   Dad's face wore an **odd** expression as he opened the door.

strange   Martha's voice sounded **strange**, and she looked frightened.

see also odd

Other words hilarious, peculiar, ridiculous, witty

Opposite words

serious   I am sorry to say I have some **serious** news.

see also sad

G

gain
see get

gather
see pick

gaze
see look

generous
see kind *and*
opposite of mean

gentle
see kind,
quiet, soft

get

get up
see rise

get *(verb)*

If you take, buy, or are given something, you **get** it: *I suggest you **get** a new pair of socks; those won't last much longer.*

become	Do you really **become** wiser as you get older?
bring	Spring often **brings** fine weather.
collect	Will you **collect** the most unusual shells you can find?
earn	Joe washes cars to **earn** money.
fetch	My dog likes to **fetch** sticks.
gain	We **gained** a lot of knowledge from our trip to the museum.
obtain	We **obtain** a lot of news from radio.
receive	We **received** a great welcome.
win	Sarah Bernhardt **won** the applause of audiences everywhere.

giggle
see laugh

give

give *(verb)*

To **give** is to hand something over to some-one for them to keep: *Please **give** me something to eat.*

bestow	The college **bestowed** the trophy on its football team.
donate	In her will, Dr. Brown **donated** a large sum of money to her old hospital.
grant	I was **granted** leave so that I could make a trip to Africa.
offer	Can I **offer** you a ride home?
present	We would like to **present** you with this gift on your retirement.
provide	Peter **provided** the food for the camping trip.
supply	We can **supply** everything you need for building your house.

Opposite words

deny	I cannot **deny** you the chance to visit Alaska.
retain	Did you **retain** part of the ticket?
withhold	Tell the whole story and don't **withhold** anything.

glad
  see happy

glide
  see slide

gloomy
  see dull, sad

go

go *(verb)*

You **go** if you advance from one place to another: *I usually go to school by bus, but I come home by car.*

continue   The road **continues** for miles.

depart   We **depart** tomorrow for Israel.

leave   What time does the plane **leave**?

move   We **moved** back to Ohio.

pass   Many years **passed** before we met again.

proceed   After lunch, we **proceeded** on our way.

travel   We **traveled** through the night and arrived home at 5 a.m.

vanish   After we left for Florida, Mary **vanished**. I never saw her again.

see also leave, turn, walk

Opposite words

stop   We **stopped** at a hotel by the sea.

see also come

good

gorge
 see eat

grab
 see catch

gradual
 see opposite of fast

grant
 see give

grasp
 see hold, take

great
 see big, important

grill
 see cook

grimy
 see dirty

grin
 see laugh

grip
 see hold

grope
 see touch

good *(adjective)*

Anything that is **good** is of high quality or the best of its kind: *Alison and John are good pupils and will do well in college.*

admirable Her behavior is **admirable**.

excellent He was a good violinist and an **excellent** pianist.

fine Here is an exclusive store which has **fine** jewelry.

fit A marvelous meal, **fit** for a king!

friendly We are lucky to have **friendly**, thoughtful neighbors.

kind She is a helpful, **kind** old lady.

pleasant New England is **pleasant** in spring.

right It's important that children are taught **right** from wrong.

sound This radio is old, but **sound**.

suitable Is Tuesday **suitable**, or would Thursday be more convenient?

see also kind, right

Other words expert, fantastic, splendid, superb, terrific

Opposite words *see* bad

grow

grow *(verb)*

If something **grows**, it becomes bigger, larger, longer, or taller: *My fingernails have grown quite long; I'll have to cut them.*

become Tom **became** tired of his old bicycle and asked for a new one.

develop Her small workshop **developed** into a factory.

enlarge This part of the map shows an **enlarged** plan of the town center.

extend My telescope **extends** to 9 inches.

increase The number of children in the school **increased** by 50.

Opposite words

decrease The number of people wearing hats has **decreased**.

see also opposite of rise

H

hamper
*see opposite
of* help

handle
see feel, touch

handsome
see beautiful

happen
see come

happy

happy *(adjective)*

If you are pleased and in a good mood, you can be called **happy**: *We went to Ben's bar mitzvah, and everyone was* **happy**.

cheerful   My brother is always **cheerful**; he's such a joker.

contented   I've finished all my work for today, and I'm **contented**.

delighted   Bill and Sue were **delighted** with their beautiful wedding presents.

glad   I'm **glad** you like my new dog.

joyful   Christmas is a **joyful** occasion, and Thanksgiving is a merry time, too.

Other words carefree, jolly, merry, satisfied

see also opposite of sad

hard

hardy
see strong

harm
see hurt

harsh
see hard *and*
opposite of kind

hasten
see hurry

haul
see pull

heal
see opposite
of hurt

heavy
see big *and*
opposite of thin

hard *(adjective)*

Anything that is not soft, or is solid, is called **hard**: *We spread the cement over the path and waited for it to get* **hard**. **Hard** can also mean "not easy to do."

awful	Somalia's civil war has made life **awful** for many.
complicated	I can't work out this problem; it's much too **complicated**.
difficult	We must save money, as there are **difficult** times ahead.
firm	The chairs were well made; **firm** and strong.
harsh	The judge is always **harsh** to criminals, and shows no mercy.
stern	My grandma is **stern**, but she is always fair.
stiff	The shoebox is made of **stiff** cardboard.
tough	I can't eat this steak; it's too **tough** and chewy!

Opposite words

mild	I always use a **mild** shampoo on my hair.

see also soft

help

helpful
 see kind

helpless
 see weak

help *(verb)*

If you do something to make life easier for someone else, you **help** them: *I like to help my parents around the house.*

aid   Harry **aided** Beth in her search for her missing earring.

assist   Carole **assisted** Jeanne with her homework.

improve   These pills will **improve** your digestion.

serve   Jo **served** the company for years.

support   Most people **supported** Dr. Stein in her search for a cure.

Opposite words

hamper   Your chatter is **hampering** my concentration.

hinder   I would have arrived earlier, but was **hindered** by the potholes in the road.

hide →

hide *(verb)*

When you **hide** something, you put it out of sight, where others cannot see it: *If you are quiet and **hide** in the bushes, you will see a lot of wildlife.*

bury   Muffin **buried** her bone in the garden.

conceal   The magician **concealed** the cards up her sleeve.

cover   At night the parrot cage is **covered** with a cloth.

disguise   Vicky **disguised** herself as a ghost for Halloween.

mask   The Moon **masks** the Sun during a solar eclipse.

Opposite words *see* find, show

59

hike
 see walk

hinder
 see opposite
 of help

hit

hit *(verb)*

If you bang or bash something hard, you can also say that you **hit** it: *The player **hit** the ball against the wall.*

beat Beat the rug to get out the dust.

bump In the dark, David **bumped** into a lamppost.

knock Somebody **knocked** on the door at midnight.

smack Sam **smacked** the naughty puppy.

strike Jill **struck** the nail with a hammer.

tap Someone **tapped** me on the arm.

thump Liz **thumped** the table in a rage.

Other words bang, bash, batter, collide, hammer, flog, whip

hold

hold *(verb)*

You **hold** something if you have it firmly in your hand: *Hold onto that rope! Help is on the way!*

clutch My little brother **clutched** my hand as we crossed the road.

contain This box **contains** pizza for lunch.

grasp Peggy **grasped** the horse's reins as it galloped out of control.

grip Gwen **gripped** the shovel and began to dig.

possess The family has **possessed** this plantation for centuries.

see also keep

Opposite word

release Sam **released** the bird from its cage.

61

Houses

Where do you live?

An adobe house
in South America

An African village
house

An Alpine chalet

A log cabin in the
forests of Canada

A trailer

A Native
American tepee

A house with a flat roof
in North America

A house on stilts in Borneo

Double words
Fill in the missing word in the center of each line, remembering that
the clues each side refer to it.

hut _ _ _ _ spill

apartment _ _ _ _ level

garden _ _ _ _ three feet

road _ _ _ method

Odd one out

The White House

Sydney Harbour Bridge

The Eiffel Tower

The Tower of Babel

A ranch-style home

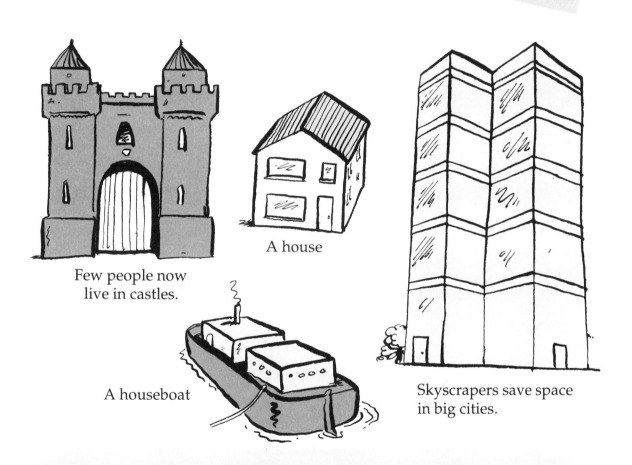

Few people now
live in castles.

A house

A houseboat

Skyscrapers save space
in big cities.

**Put in the missing letters to make a word that is the name of a
part of a house:**

w _ n _ ow   do _ r   c _ imn _ y   roo _   f _ o _ r

wa _ l   ce _ l _ ng   st _ i _ s

honest
  see right

hot
  see opposite
  of cold

huge
  see big

humorous
  see funny

hurry

hurry *(verb)*

If you **hurry**, you move or do something quickly, often because there's not enough time: *Please **hurry** with my breakfast, I have to catch a train.*

dash	The naughty dog **dashed** after the frightened cat.
hasten	José **hastened** his step to keep up with the others.
race	Jo **raced** to the phone as it rang.
run	Look at the ants! They **run** in all directions.
rush	The ambulance **rushed** to the hospital.
speed	Howard was stopped for **speeding** down the highway.

see also run

Opposite words

dawdle	Stop **dawdling** and catch up!
delay	All flights are **delayed** because of ice and snow.
linger	After the reception, the guests **lingered** in the lobby.

hurt

hush
see opposite of noise

hushed
see quiet

hurt *(verb)*

When you **hurt** somebody you cause them pain or distress: *What you said was very cruel, and it **hurt** me a lot.*

ache   The din makes my ears **ache**.

damage   The town was **damaged** by the earthquake.

harm   Did the wolf **harm** the hens?

injure   Rachel **injured** her back in a riding accident.

upset   Watching the sad movie **upset** Henry.

wound   Fred was **wounded** in battle and has a bad limp.

Opposite words

console   After her kitten died, nothing could **console** our poor cat.

heal   This cream will **heal** anything!

soothe   What a **soothing** voice you have.

I

illustration
see picture

important

improper
see opposite of right

improve
see help

impure
see dirty

incorrect
see wrong

increase
see grow, rise

indicate
see mean, show

indignant
see angry

important *(adjective)*

Something that is serious and matters a great deal is said to be **important**: *This book gives a list of the most **important** dates in history.*

famous Greta Garbo was a **famous** Hollywood star.

great La Scala in Milan is one of the world's **great** opera houses.

main The **main** cities of Zimbabwe are Harare and Bulawayo.

necessary Water is **necessary** for all life.

Opposite words

minor **Minor** and miner sound the same but have a **minor** spelling difference.

petty **Petty** details are unimportant.

66

injure
  see hurt

inquire
  see ask

insist
  see say

inspect
  see see

intelligent
  see clever

intend
  see mean

interesting

introduce
  see start

invent
  see make

invite
  see ask

irate
  see angry

interesting *(adjective)*

Something that holds your attention, or that you want to know more about, is **interesting**: *This magazine has an **interesting** article on the Ainu people of Japan.*

entertaining She has such **entertaining** stories about the old days.

fascinating Sharon finds ancient Egyptian history **fascinating**.

pleasing What a **pleasing** view of the old church.

Opposite words *see* dull

J

job
see work

join

jostle
see push

joyful
see happy

just
see fair, right

join *(verb)*

When you **join** things, you put them together: *To splice, you **join** two short pieces of rope to make one long one.* **Join** can also mean "to become a member of": *We **joined** the football team.*

connect The tunnel **connects** New York and New Jersey.

fasten Judy **fastened** the papers together with a stapler.

link The trailer is **linked** to the tractor.

unite We all **united** to fight the enemy.

Opposite words

disconnect When we moved, the telephone was **disconnected**.

separate Sudan is **separated** from Saudi Arabia by the Red Sea.

keep *(verb)*

If you have something, and do not give it to someone else, you **keep** it: *I shall always keep this ring; it will remind me of you.*

continue I'm too tired to **continue** playing.

hold Catherine **held** the coins.

observe The first of May is **observed** in many countries as a holiday.

retain I **retain** a vivid memory of what he looked like.

save **Save** this coupon for a free gift!

see also hold

Opposite words

discard I **discarded** my winter clothes.

forsake My father loved cigars, but decided to **forsake** smoking altogether.

throw away Please **throw away** that rubbish!

kind *(adjective)*

Kind people are always ready to help others: *Anthony is **kind** to all animals.*

generous   Judy is **generous** and always shares her candy.

gentle   Jim gave his friend a **gentle** hug.

helpful   You've been very **helpful** showing me the way.

tender   I gave my puppy a **tender** look.

see also good

Opposite words

harsh   The angry salesclerk spoke to us in **harsh** words.

severe   There are **severe** laws in Peru.

see also hard

kindle
 see light

knock
 see hit

know

know *(verb)*

If you **know** something, it is in your mind and you are aware of what it is about: *She always knows all the answers.*

recall   I **recall** his face very well, but I've forgotten his name!

recognize I didn't **recognize** you in those dark glasses.

understand I lived in Japan for a year, so I **understand** Japanese.

see also think

Same sound

no   (*adjective*) There's **no** knowing what will happen.

L

labor
see work

lamp
see light

large
see big *and*
opposite of small

laugh

laugh *(verb)*

When you hear, see, or think of something funny, you **laugh**: *The Marx Brothers made nearly everyone **laugh**.*

chuckle   Laura **chuckled** to herself as she read the funny book.

giggle   He told a lot of silly jokes, but they made us all **giggle**.

grin   Louise **grinned** when Jim gave her a present.

smile   **Smile** and the whole world **smiles** with you.

snicker   Some people **snickered** when Joe slipped on the banana peel, but I didn't think it was funny.

Opposite words

cry   The sad story made Chris **cry**.

launch
  see send

lay
  see put

lean
  see thin

leave

leave *(verb)*

If you go away from somewhere, you **leave**:
*I have to **leave** New York tomorrow, as I'm due in Tokyo on Monday.*

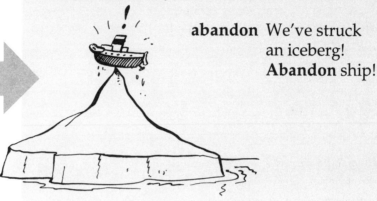

abandon We've struck an iceberg! **Abandon** ship!

depart   We're going to Jamaica and we **depart** from Miami.

desert   Paul Gauguin, the artist, **deserted** his family and went to the South Seas.

forsake Joe has **forsaken** his old carefree life and become a Buddhist monk.

quit   After 20 years, he **quit** the circus and settled down.

see also go

Opposite words

arrive   My family **arrived** to meet me when I stepped off the plane.

see also come

Land names

Which of these features can you see on this page?
continent isthmus plateau / ocean sea bay gulf / beach coast
sand shore / cliff precipice / valley canyon fjord gorge /
river wadi stream brook burn delta estuary /
hill mountain slope range elevation mount /
desert tundra wasteland dune / forest wood
copse spinney jungle / savanna steppes
pampas plain grasslands prairie /
coral reef / bush outback / oasis
watering hole / island isle
peninsula / marsh bog
swamp quicksand /
volcano geyser

Hidden rivers
Find the rivers hidden in these sentences. Look for
letters that follow each other.
1. Soon I leave this country for a boat tour of the world.
2. After the first thud, sonic boom waves were blamed
   for the damage.
3. When meat is used with spaghetti, gristle, fat, and
   bone must be removed.

What animal lives in which land feature?
camel kangaroo eagle cattle squirrel dolphin

Same sound

beach / *beech*   steppes / *steps*

shore / *sure*   wood / *would*

isle / *I'll, aisle*   sea / *see*

Say it either way

Niagara, O roar again

Able was I, ere I saw Elba

level
   see smooth

light

light *(adjective)*

If something is not heavy and has very little weight, we say that it's **light**: *I'll carry your bag for you; it's as **light** as a feather.* **Light** is also the power that makes it possible for us to see things: *The Sun gives off bright **light**.*

airy	*Full of fresh air and breezes:* What a bright and **airy** room!
buoyant	The rubber dinghy was **buoyant**, floating about on the waves.
flimsy	The hut was so **flimsy** that the wind blew it down one night.
pale	Her dress was pink, or perhaps you could call it **pale** red.
kindle	*(verb) To light a fire:* **Kindle** those sticks and we'll soon have a fire.
lamp	*(noun)* We like to keep the **lamp** lit on the porch.

see also fair

Other words *(verb)* burn, flare, ignite, illuminate, gleam, glitter, sparkle

like

like *(verb)*

If you think a person or thing is pleasant, then you **like** it: *I **like** most sweet things, but my favorite is chocolate.*

admire   I **admire** doctors and nurses because they help sick people.

love   I **love** being by the sea.

prefer   I play many sports, but I **prefer** basketball.

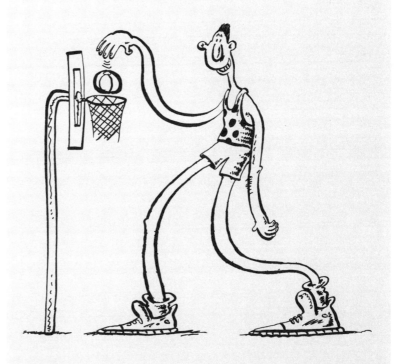

see also love

linger
see opposite
of hurry

link
see join

little
see small *and*
opposite of big

load
see put

locate
see find

lock
see shut

lonely

lonesome
see lonely

lonely *(adjective)*

If you are on your own, without friends, you can say that you are **lonely**: *Big cities are full of people, but you can feel **lonely** there.*

alone   Robinson Crusoe lived all **alone** on a desert island.

friendless   I was quite **friendless** when I arrived in the big city.

lonesome   Abdul felt **lonesome** and home-sick in that distant country.

solitary   As I crossed the field, I saw just one **solitary** house.

look *(verb)*

When you use your eyes to see something, you **look**: *Look at the sunset; it's beautiful.*

gaze Sarah **gazed** at the butterflies.

notice Have you ever **noticed** Neil's knobby knees?

regard The professor **regarded** her students through thick-lensed glasses.

see He shaded his eyes to **see** across the rippling water.

seem Larry **seems** to be younger than he really is.

stare I **stared** with horror as the scorpion crawled nearer.

watch **Watch** out for a number 22 bus.

see also see

lose
*see opposite
of* find

loud

loud *(adjective)*

If something makes a lot of noise, we say that it is **loud**: *Turn down the radio, please; it's too loud and is giving me a headache.*

boisterous   The quiet town was invaded by **boisterous** football fans.

noisy   It was a **noisy** meeting, and we had to shout to be heard.

raucous   That harsh, **raucous** noise is Ted practicing on his trumpet.

showy   He wore a **showy**, large-patterned suit.

shrill   The **shrill** sound of a whistle is earsplitting.

see also noisy

Opposite words *see* quiet, soft

love

lovely
  see beautiful

love *(verb)*

If you have a strong liking for, or a great attraction to, something or someone, you can use the word **love**: *I **love** my family with all my heart*.

adore   Guy **adores** his grandfather.

like   I **like** most kinds of music.

worship   Warren **worships** his uncle.

affection   (*noun*) I have a great **affection** for all animals.

esteem   (*noun*) The author of that book is held in high **esteem** by her readers.

see also like

M

mad
see angry

main
see important

make

make *(verb)*

If we **make** something, we put other things together, or create it: *Jack just **made** a crane with his construction set.* **Make** can also mean "to cause something to happen."

build   I'm **building** a tree house.

compel   It rained so much, we were **compelled** to stay at home.

construct   Ann learned how to **construct** a model car.

earn   How much do you **earn** in your new job?

form   We **formed** a society for those interested in painting.

invent   Printing was **invented** by the Chinese.

manufacture   The Koreans **manufacture** cars and bikes.

mold   The potter **molded** a pot out of the clay.

prepare   Dad **prepared** dinner for us.

Opposite words

destroy   The storm **destroyed** the boat.

undo   Can you **undo** the knot?

82

manufacture
see make

many

many *(adjective)*

If you have a large number of something, then you could say you have **many**: *Were there **many** children in class today?*

frequent   Mark makes **frequent** visits to our house. He comes several times a week.

numerous   We advertised in the local paper and had **numerous** replies.

Opposite words

few   **Few** people like snakes.

rare   Butterflies are **rare** in Greenland.

march
  see walk

mask
  see hide

mean

mediocre
  see fair

mend
  see opposite
  of break

mean *(verb)*

When we **mean** something, we show it, are serious about it, or explain it: *Dictionaries are books that tell us what words **mean***. **Mean** as an *adjective* can describe someone who is not generous.

indicate The hands on a clock **indicate** what time it is.

intend I **intend** to go to the zoo tomorrow.

nasty (*adjective*) Meg said **nasty**, spiteful things about her boss.

stingy (*adjective*) Scrooge had always been miserly and **stingy**, but later was kind to Tiny Tim.

unkind (*adjective*) It was selfish and **unkind** of you not to ask Clara to your party.

Opposite word

generous Ruth is very successful but she's always **generous** to her staff.

mess

mild
see quiet *and*
opposite of hard

mingle
see mix

minor
see opposite
of important

minute
see small

miserable
see sad

miss
see opposite
of catch

mistaken
see wrong

misty
see opposite
of clear

mess *(noun)*

If someone or something is in a **mess**, they are dirty, untidy, or mixed up: *This room is a complete **mess**.*

clutter   In the closet there was a **clutter** of old clothes.

difficulty   She got into **difficulty** and had to be rescued.

muddle   My brain is in a **muddle**. I don't remember where I put my keys.

Music

Instruments around the world

In every part of the world people play musical instruments. Some instruments have remained unchanged for hundreds of years; others, like the steel drum of the West Indies, made from oil drums, are recent.

Steel drums from the West Indies

Bagpipes
from Scotland

Banjo from the United States

Panpipes from
South America

Musical memory
Mnemonics (pronounced nem on ics), or memory aids, are named after the Greek goddess of memory, Mnemosyne. Here are two musical examples: The lines and spaces of the treble stave in written music are: E F G A B C D E F; those of the bass stave are G A B C D E F G A. These silly sentences may help you remember them: **E**very **F**ine **G**irl **A**nd **B**oy **C**an **D**efinitely **E**at **F**ish and **G**ood **A**nd **B**ad **C**ats **D**on't **E**ver **F**ind **G**reen **A**nts.

Sound the same
band	banned
reed (*of a pipe*)	read
keys (*of a piano*)	quays (*in a port*)
cymbals (*you hit*)	symbols (*signs*)

Sound different
bass	bass
(*deep male voice*)	(*a kind of fish*)
bow	bow
(*of a violin*)	(*a greeting*)

Songs with different tunes
song anthem carol hymn lullaby
pop song nursery rhyme

Groups of Instruments

In an orchestra there are four main groups of instruments:
strings instruments that are plucked or played with a bow.
woodwind instruments made of wood or metal. The player blows into or across the mouthpiece.
brass instruments made of metal.
percussion instruments that are hit or shaken.

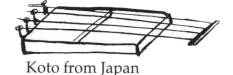

See if you can place these instruments in the right group:

harp violin clarinet xylophone cello guitar tambourine double bass oboe gong trumpet trombone

Didgeridoo from Australia

Koto from Japan

Sitar from India

Gamelan orchestra from Indonesia

Balalaika from Russia

mix

modern
see opposite of old

modify
see change

moist
see wet

moisten
see wet

mold
see make

move
see go

muddle
see mess

mix *(verb)*

If you put things together, or shake them, you **mix** them: *To make the cake, put all the ingredients together and* **mix** *them in a bowl.*

blend   You **blend** flour and water to make paste.

combine   The orchestra and chorus were **combined** for a special performance.

mingle   It was a great party; everyone **mingled** quite happily.

shuffle   Please **shuffle** the cards.

stir   Sue **stirred** her coffee.

N

name
see call

narrow
see thin

nasty
see bad, mean,
and opposite
of nice

naughty
see bad

nearly
see about

necessary
see important

nervous
see afraid

new
see opposite
of old

nibble
see eat

nice

nice *(adjective)*

Someone or something you like or find attractive, is **nice**: *I would like a **nice** cool drink. She's a very **nice** girl. Isn't it **nice** here?*

comfortable   The kittens are sleeping on a cozy, **comfortable** cushion.

delicious   This plum is **delicious**!

enjoyable   Summer camp was **enjoyable**.

pleasant   We spent a **pleasant** week in a charming Swiss village.

smart   What **smart**, stylish, and elegant clothes they wear!

thoughtful   It was **thoughtful** and kind of you to look after my dog.

see also beautiful, fair, good, interesting, kind

Opposite words

nasty   That's a **nasty** cut.

rude   It's **rude** to say, "Shut up."

noise

noisy
see loud *and*
opposite of quiet

normal
see opposite
of odd

notice
see look, see

numerous
see many

noise *(noun)*

We sometimes speak of **noise** when what we hear is loud and unpleasant: *We live near the airport, and the aircraft **noise** is terrible.*

clamor   A hundred people all talking at once makes quite a **clamor** in a small room.

din   There was such a **din**, I couldn't hear myself talk.

racket   This morning the crows were making an awful **racket**.

sound   **Sounds** can be loud and deafening, or soft and soothing.

Opposite words

hush   There was a **hush** when the teacher appeared.

silence   I need complete **silence** to be able to concentrate.

O

observe
  see keep, see

obtain
  see get

obvious
  see clear, plain

occupied
  see opposite
  of empty

occur
  see come

odd

odd *(adjective)*

If something is **odd**, it is not ordinary or usual: *The Horny Goloch sounds like a very* **odd** *animal.* Or, it can mean "left over," "not even," or "not alike": *I always seem to have several* **odd** *socks. Two is an even number, three is an* **odd** *one.*

peculiar   It's **peculiar** for a lobster to blow its nose.

quaint   There are many **quaint** villages in Mexico.

strange   I had a **strange** dream about a weird worm.

unusual   It's **unusual** to see an octopus knitting.

see also funny

Opposite words

even   Four is an **even** number.

normal   It's **normal** to want to play outside on a sunny day.

usual   I went the **usual** way home.

offer
  see give

old

open
  see start

operate
  see work

oppose
  see fight

ordinary
  see plain

old *(adjective)*

Anyone who has lived for a long time, or anything that has existed for a long time, is **old**: *This armchair is very **old**; it was my great-grandmother's.*

aged　　Professor Mills looks after her **aged** mother.

ancient　Excavations in Benin showed relics of the **ancient** civilization.

antique　My uncle is interested in really old things, and collects **antique** silver.

worn　　You should buy a new jacket; that one is shabby and **worn**.

Opposite words

modern　The computer is a **modern** invention.

new　　**New** leaves come out in spring.

recent　What's the most **recent** news?

young　All **young** animals are cute.

P

packed
see full
and opposite
of empty

painting
see picture

pal
see friend

pale
see light

panic
see fright

parched
see dry
and opposite
of wet

part
see piece

pass
see go

peaceful
see calm, quiet

peculiar
see odd

peer
see see

performance
see show

petty
see opposite
of important

photograph
see picture

pick *(verb)*

pick

If you **pick** something, you remove it or you decide to take it from a selection offered to you: *Pick one of these cards.*

choose   Brenda **chose** the biggest piece of cake.

gather   Let's go out and **gather** some logs for our winter fires.

pluck   Jeff **plucked** an apple from the tree and began to munch on it.

select   Jane **selected** some tomatoes and walked to the checkout counter.

picture

picture *(noun)*

If you put an image on paper or other surface, you make a **picture**: *I like books with plenty of pictures in them.*

drawing A **drawing** is a picture in pen or pencil.

illustration This book has color **illustrations**.

painting The Mona Lisa is the most famous **painting** in the world.

photograph Kay used her new camera to take a **photograph** of the giraffe.

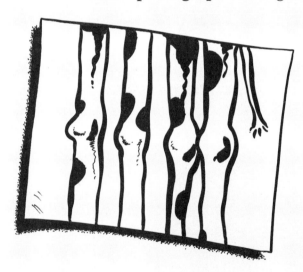

portrait This is a **portrait** of my great-aunt.

sketch Mustapha did a quick **sketch** of the new mosque.

piece

place
see put

placid
see calm

piece *(noun)*

A small section of something is called a **piece**: *That chocolate cake looks delicious. May I have a piece?*

bit Look at my vase! It's broken into tiny **bits**.

fragment The window smashed, and **fragments** of glass flew everywhere.

part This **part** of the building is used as a library.

portion After the duke died, a large **portion** of his lands became a public garden.

Other words chip, chunk, portion, slice, splinter

Same sound

peace My brother needs **peace** and quiet to study.

plain

pleasant
see good, nice

pleased
see opposite
of angry

pleasing
see interesting

pliable
see soft

pluck
see pick

plunge
see push

poke
see push

polished
see smooth

polluted
see dirty

portion
see piece

portrait
see picture

plain *(adjective)*

Something that is not complicated, and has no decoration, is called **plain**: *Jill made good furniture; it was **plain** but strong.* **Plain** can also mean "not pretty." As a *noun*, it means a large area of flat, open land.

frank	I'll give you a **frank** reply: I didn't like the play at all.
obvious	The answer to this easy question is **obvious**.
ordinary	Andy's just an **ordinary** fellow; he doesn't try to be clever.
simple	This is an old-fashioned village, and we all live **simple** lives.

see also clear

Same sound

plane	*(noun)* The **plane** landed early.

Opposite word

complicated	I can't do algebra; it's much too **complicated** for me.

possess
see hold

powerful
see strong

prefer
  see like

prepare
  see make

present
  see give

press
  see push

pretty
  see beautiful

proceed
  see go

pronounce
  see say

propel
  see push

proper
  see right *and*
  opposite of wrong

provide
  see give

prune
  see cut

pull →

pull *(verb)*

If you get hold of something and make it come toward you, you **pull** it: *In the old days, steam locomotives were used to **pull** trains.*

drag   Debra helped Isabel **drag** the desk across the room.

draw   Black horses are used to **draw** the queen's coach.

haul   We must all **haul** on this rope to bring up the sail.

stretch   I **stretched** the rope across the yard to make a clothesline.

tug   He **tugged** hard at the knob, but he couldn't open the door.

Other words
heave, tow

Opposite words
see push

Plants

All flowering plants have the same four main parts: roots, stems, leaves, flowers. Most make new plants by growing seeds. Nonflowering plants can't make seeds. They make new plants with spores (tiny cells). Mosses and bracken are non-flowering plants, and so is seaweed.

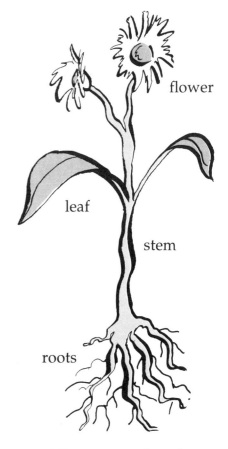

flower

leaf

stem

roots

The parts of a plant

Fruit, flower, vegetable, or tree?

Group these plants and put them in the correct alphabetical order:

pear	bean
elm	iris
apple	pea
grape	daffodil
lettuce	celery
beech	pineapple
onion	daisy
avocado	cauliflower
nut	lemon
lily	oak
carrot	cassava
tulip	nasturtium

A weather forecasting rhyme

Oak before ash
You're in for a splash.
Ash before oak
You're in for a soak.

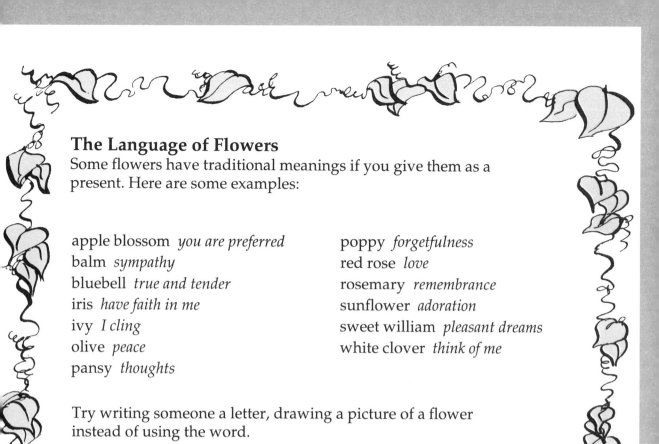

The Language of Flowers

Some flowers have traditional meanings if you give them as a present. Here are some examples:

apple blossom *you are preferred*
balm *sympathy*
bluebell *true and tender*
iris *have faith in me*
ivy *I cling*
olive *peace*
pansy *thoughts*

poppy *forgetfulness*
red rose *love*
rosemary *remembrance*
sunflower *adoration*
sweet william *pleasant dreams*
white clover *think of me*

Try writing someone a letter, drawing a picture of a flower instead of using the word.

Some plant homonyms

bough / *bow*
beech / *beach*
berry / *bury*
cereal / *serial*
currant / *current*
fir / *fur*
flower / *flour*
lichen / *liken*
plum / *plumb*
rye / *wry*
thyme / *time*
weed / *we'd*
wood / *would*

Roots

Can you complete these words without using a dictionary?

geran _ _ _   tu _ _ _   da _ _ _

    dandel _ _ _   chrysan _ _ _ _ _ _

sunflo _ _ _   marigo _ _   wallf _ _ _ _ _

puny
  see small, weak

pure
  see clear

push

push *(verb)*

If you apply force to something to make it move away from you, you **push** it: *Tim's car broke down on a hill, so we all had to get out and push it.*

force Angela had lost her key, so she had to **force** her suitcase open.

jostle When the big parade went by, we were **jostled** by the crowds.

plunge We **plunged** through the driving snow.

poke Our ball got lodged in a drainpipe, but I **poked** it out.

press **Press** the button to start.

propel Someone pushed me from behind, and **propelled** me forward.

thrust Mark **thrust** several coins into his pocket.

Other words bump, cram, nudge, shove

Opposite words *see* pull

put

put *(verb)*

When you move something into position, you **put** it there: *All our warm clothes were **put** away for the summer.*

deposit   I **deposited** my hat and coat in the cloakroom.

lay   **Lay** all your cards on the table.

load   Larry **loaded** the washing machine.

place   She **placed** her foot firmly on the first step of the ladder.

set   Jill **set** a heavy package on the table.

stand   **Stand** that clock on the shelf.

stick   Our dog always **sticks** its head out of the car window.

Opposite words

remove   I must ask you to **remove** all this clutter immediately.

withdraw   We went to the bank and **withdrew** enough money to pay for my bicycle.

Q

quaint
  see odd

quarrel
  see fight

query
  see ask

quick
  see fast

quiet

quit
  see leave

quiver
  see shake

quiet *(adjective)*

When there is no sound or noise, it is **quiet**: *The house was so **quiet** that it seemed rather spooky.*

calm	The storm had blown over, and now the sea was **calm**.
gentle	Alison has a **gentle**, soothing voice.
mild	Johnny is a **mild**, sweet person.
peaceful	After the war, we all looked forward to **peaceful** times.
silent	We stood **silent**, looking at the deer.
tranquil	I went for a walk at dawn, a very **tranquil** time.

see also calm, soft, *and opposite of* loud

Other words hushed, shy, timid

Opposite words

disturbing	The constant banging of the door is very **disturbing**.
noisy	My sleep was broken by the **noisy** seagulls.

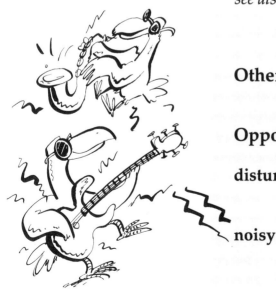

R

race
see hurry, run

racket
see noise

rainy
see wet

rapid
see fast

rare
see opposite of many

rash
see opposite of careful

raucous
see loud

reasonable
see fair

recall
see know

receive
see get *and opposite of* send

recent
see opposite of old

recite
see say

recognize
see know

reconcile
see opposite of fight

regard
see look

reject
see opposite of take

relax
see rest

release
see opposite of catch, hold

remainder
see rest

remark
see say

remove
see opposite of put

repair
see opposite of break

reply
see say

repose
see rest

request
see ask

rest

rest *(verb)*

If you are working hard, you might stop to **rest**: *We've been walking for hours; we ought to rest*. **Rest** as a *noun* also means "what is left over": *I've eaten most of the cherries, but you can have the* **rest**.

relax   Emma has been exercising very hard. Now she must **relax**.

repose   The actress **reposed** on the recliner, pretending to be asleep.

sleep   I lay on the sofa and **slept**.

remainder *(noun)* Some children went home for lunch, but the **remainder** ate sandwiches at school.

Other words *(noun)* remnant, residue, *(verb)* slumber, snooze

retain
see keep *and*
opposite of
change, give

reveal
see show

right

right *(adjective)*

When we speak of the **right** thing, we mean the correct, true, or best thing: *Is this the **right** road for Jane's house?* **Right** is also the opposite of left.

correct	Do you have the **correct** time?
good	If you need a wristwatch, I'll buy you a **good** one.
honest	I'll be **honest** with you; I don't like this food.
just	It was only **just** that Tina should get the job rather than Bill.
proper	Before we can do the repairs, we must have the **proper** tools.
suitable	Is this scarf **suitable** for summer?
upright	Everyone trusts the rabbi, for he is an **upright**, good person.

see also fair, good

Opposite words

false	I'm sorry, but these papers are **false**. Someone forged them.
improper	Those boots are quite **improper** for ballet dancing!

see also wrong

105

rise *(verb)*

If you stand up, or go upward, you **rise**:
*Everyone **rises** when the judge enters the court.*
*The balloon began to **rise** slowly.*

ascend	We **ascended** the long, winding stairway to the attic.
float	Jenny watched the bubbles **float** away.
get up	Hurry! It's time to **get up**!
increase	Our prices will **increase** from tomorrow.
soar	The eagle **soared** into the sky.

Other words climb, stand up, take off

Opposite words

decline	She's not well; her health has **declined** over the last year.
decrease	Our speed **decreased** to a snail's pace.
descend	She **descended** the slope to meet the rescue party.
sink	The Sun **sinks** in the west.

roast
  see cook

robust
  see strong

rotten
  see bad

rough

rough *(adjective)*

If something is not smooth, or is wild and noisy, we say it is **rough**: *We can't drive our car over the bumpy, **rough** ground.*

boisterous   They don't mean any harm; they're just rowdy, **boisterous** children.

coarse   The prisoners wore uniforms made of **coarse** material.

crude   The first tools were quite **crude**.

rugged   The mountain road is **rugged**.

stormy   The sea was **stormy** and everyone felt seasick.

uneven   It's an old house, with **uneven** floors and ceilings.

Same sound

ruff   *(noun)* The circus poodle wore a fancy **ruff** around its neck.

Opposite words

delicate   The **delicate** cloth is trimmed with fine lace.

smooth   Stir the paint until it's **smooth**.

soft   Hank stroked the cat's **soft** fur.

107

rude
see opposite of nice

rugged
see rough

run

rush
see hurry

run *(verb)*

When you move your legs quickly to take you along the ground, you **run**: *Run and call for help.*

dash	I **dashed** after my grandmother, as she had forgotten her keys.
flow	The syrup **flowed** into the bowl.
hurry	You'll have to **hurry** to catch her.
race	We cheered the winner as she **raced** past the finish line.

sprint	Jan **sprinted** across the field like a little antelope.
trot	Horses walk, **trot**, canter, or gallop; humans walk, jog, or run.

see also hurry

sad *(adjective)*

People are **sad** when something has happened that upsets them: *Tim was* **sad** *when his cat died.*

depressed So many things went wrong, and we all felt **depressed**.

dismal The sunshine did not reach the **dismal** street.

gloomy Why are you so **gloomy**?

miserable I've been **miserable** without you.

sorrowful Charles Dickens wrote of the **sorrowful** plight of the poor.

unhappy Sue was **unhappy** when Simon went away.

Other words glum, heartbroken, tragic

Opposite words

cheerful She's a **cheerful** girl; she's always smiling.

happy We're **happy** to hear your good news.

see also funny, happy

save
see keep

saw
see cut

say

say *(verb)*

When you **say** something, you use your voice to make sounds, or express thoughts in writing: *What did her mother* **say** *about it? What does the paper* **say** *about the weather?*

declare   I **declare** that I will not sell this house.

exclaim   "What a strange hat!" **exclaimed** Ginny.

insist   Don **insisted** that we'd met before.

pronounce   How do you **pronounce** "last"?

recite   Jack **recited** a funny poem to the guests.

remark   Dad **remarked** on the room's neatness.

reply   "Never," I heard him **reply**.

speak   I can **speak** a little Spanish.

suggest   I **suggest** we all go for a swim.

tell   Please **tell** me what's the matter!

utter   I was so surprised that I couldn't **utter** a word.

Other words announce, express, mention, murmur, mutter, shout, state, whisper, yell

scared
  see afraid

seal
  see shut

secure
  see fast, strong

see

see *(verb)*

If we **see**, we recognize or distinguish something with our eyes: *I **see** a group of people coming toward us. Can you **see** what's on the label?*

inspect   Sherlock Holmes **inspected** the letter through his magnifying glass.

notice   I **notice** that you've come on your bicycle.

observe   **Observe** how the horse moves.

peer   We **peered** through the crack.

understand Now I **understand** why you wanted to leave early.

watch   **Watch** carefully, and I'll make this box disappear!

see also look

Same sound

sea   (*noun*) The sailors were at **sea** for two weeks without seeing land.

seem
see look

seize
see take

select
see pick

send

send *(verb)*

To **send** is to cause something or someone to move or be moved from one place to another: *I'll **send** you a letter tomorrow. I'll **send** my brother to pick you up.*

convey   Please **convey** my best wishes to your parents.

dispatch   Colonel Briggs **dispatched** his report.

launch   The rocket was **launched** into space.

mail   This letter was **mailed** yesterday.

transmit   The radio operator **transmitted** a distress call immediately.

Opposite words

receive   I **received** lots of gifts on my birthday.

see also get

sense
 see feel

separate
 see opposite
 of join

serious
 see opposite
 of funny

serve
 see help

set
 see put

severe
 see opposite
 of kind

shake

sharp
 see opposite
 of dull

shatter
 see break

shiver
 see shake

short
 see small

shake *(verb)*

You **shake** something if you move it up and down or from side to side with short, quick movements: *Before you open the bottle, **shake** it well. The bus **shook** as it drove over the railroad tracks.*

flutter   We watched the flag **flutter**.

quiver   Kerry **quivered** with excitement as she entered the circus tent.

shiver   We all **shivered** with cold.

shudder   Seeing the spider in the bathtub made me **shudder**!

sway   Our boat **swayed** from side to side.

tremble   The thunder made the dog **tremble**.

vibrate   The building **vibrated** as the airliner swept over it.

shout
see call

show

show *(verb)*

If you allow or cause something to be seen, or make it visible, you **show** it: *Let me **show** you our garden.*

demonstrate The manager **demonstrated** the new washing machine.

display Many gifts were **displayed**.

expose My face is quite sore after being **exposed** to the wind.

indicate He spoke no English, but pointed to **indicate** what he wanted.

reveal She smiled, **revealing** a row of shining white teeth.

teach Could you **teach** me how to operate the computer?

performance *(noun)* I saw a marvelous **performance** at the opera.

Other words *(noun)* exhibition, fair, film, play

showy
see loud

shrill
see loud

shudder
see shake

shuffle
see mix

shut

shy
see quiet *and*
opposite of bold

silence
see opposite
of noise

silent
see quiet

silky
see soft

simple
see clear, plain

shut *(verb)*

If you move something to cover an opening,
or place a cover on something, you **shut** it:
*Please **shut** the door as you go out.*

bar   We tried to cross the bridge, but
a herd of cattle **barred** our way.

close   **Close** your eyes and imagine
you are back in the Middle Ages.

fasten   Somebody had **fastened** the old
chest with iron bands.

lock   I've **locked** all the doors.

seal   I placed the letter in an envelope
and **sealed** it carefully.

closed   *(adjective)* By the time we reached
town, all the stores were **closed**.

sink
  see fall *and*
  opposite of rise

sketch
  see picture

skid
  see slide

skill
  see touch

skillful
  see able

skinny
  see thin

sleek
  see smooth

sleep
  see rest

slender
  see thin

slice
  see cut

slide

slide *(verb)*

You **slide** if you move, or cause something to move, smoothly over a surface: *You don't have to push these doors; they* **slide** *open.*

glide   The music floated across the hall as the dancers **glided** by.

skid   I applied the brakes, and the car **skidded** on the slippery road.

slip   The soap **slipped** out of my hands.

slither   The snake **slithered** through the long grass.

slight
see small

slip
see slide

slither
see slide

slow
see opposite of fast

smack
see hit

small

small *(adjective)*

Something that is not large, is **small**: *Only a small number of people live in our town.*

little	The **little** boy lost his dad in the crowd.
minute	The words were so **minute** that we needed a magnifying glass to read them.
puny	In olden times, children were often **puny** because they weren't fed properly.
short	Dachshunds have **short** legs.
slight	Mary is **slight** and delicate.
tiny	We lifted a stone, and lots of **tiny** creatures scurried away.
trivial	It's not important, just a **trivial** matter.
unimportant	It's an **unimportant** flaw in the design.

Opposite words

large	We have a small house, but it has a **large** garden.

see also big

smart *see* nice	

smash
see break

smile
see laugh

smooth

snatch
see take

snicker
see laugh

snip
see cut

soak
see wet

soar
see rise

smooth *(adjective)*

When something has a surface that is free from rough parts, dents, or lumps, we say it is **smooth**: *The tide has gone out, and the sand looks **smooth**.*

even The ship continued through the seas at an **even** speed.

flat The land is **flat** around here; there isn't a hill for miles.

level See how **level** the lawn is after I used our new roller.

polished That **polished** table top looks just like glass.

sleek The panther's **sleek** fur gleams.

Other words calm, creamy, silky

Opposite words *see* rough

soft

soiled
see dirty

solid
see strong

solitary
see lonely

soothe
see opposite of hurt

sorrowful
see sad

sound
see good, noise

sour
see bad

sparse
see thin

speak
see say, talk

speech
see talk

speed
see hurry

spin
see turn

soft *(adjective)*

Anything that is easy to mold, press, or dent is called **soft**: *This bed has a lovely soft mattress.*

delicate	What **delicate** wings butterflies have!
fluffy	The hens' eggs have hatched, and now there are dozens of **fluffy** chicks.
gentle	A warm, **gentle** breeze was blowing.
pliable	This modeling clay needs warming to make it **pliable**.
quiet	The children whispered in **quiet** voices.
silky	Her hair was soft and **silky**.

see also quiet *and opposite of* loud, rough

Opposite words *see* hard

Sport

A B C of sports

Archery badminton baseball basketball billiards
bowling boxing canoeing cricket curling darts
fencing football high jump hockey horseback riding
judo karate lacrosse long jump luge pelota
pole vault polo pool real tennis rodeo rowing rugby
running sailing shooting skating skiing soccer
softball squash stadium jumping swimming
table tennis tennis tobogganing water polo
waterskiing wrestling

Sound the same

cricket (*game*)	cricket (*insect*)
ball	bawl (*yell*)
bowled (*rolled a ball*)	bold (*daring*)
links (*where golf is played*)	lynx (*catlike animal*)

Pairing

Match the following three-letter groups to make six-letter words connected with sport.

kar soc ten pel box rid ski run jum arr hoc

ing ing ner ows per key ate nis cer ota ing

Here are some main divisions of sport.
Can you group all the sports on these pages?

combat sports (e.g. boxing)   water sports

track and field   court games

target sports   goal sports

cue sports   bat and ball games

winter sports   equestrian events

121

split
see break

sprint
see run

stand
see put

stare
see look

start

steal
see take

step
see walk

stern
see hard

stew
see cook

stick
see put

stiff
see hard

still
see calm

stingy
see mean

start *(verb)*

When something **starts**, it is set in motion, or happens for the first time: *I **started** a new job this morning, so I set my alarm clock to wake me up early.*

begin	The Pilgrims went to America to **begin** a new life.
commence	The show **commences** at eight o'clock.
establish	We **established** our company over 40 years ago.
introduce	They are going to **introduce** a new TV show tonight.
open	The story **opens** in 1715.

Opposite words *see* end

stint	
see turn	
stir	
see mix	
stop	
see opposite of go	
stormy	
see rough *and opposite of* calm	
strange	
see funny, odd	
stretch	
see pull	
stride	
see walk	
strike	
see hit	
strive	
see try	
stroll	
see walk	
strong	
struggle	
see fight	

strong *(adjective)*

If you are **strong**, you have great power and are able to do things that need energy: *In some countries, **strong** animals, such as oxen, are used to pull carts.*

brawny	He had large muscles on his **brawny** arms.
firm	The firefighters held on to the hose with a **firm** grip.
hardy	Farmers are tough and **hardy**.
powerful	The apes were **powerful** enough to uproot trees.
robust	The athletes are young and **robust**.
secure	Gold is stored in **secure** vaults.
solid	The house was built on a **solid** rock foundation.
sturdy	That is a **sturdy** old oak tree.
tough	The mast was held in position by **tough** cables.

see also able

Other words enthusiastic, unbreakable, violent, vivid

Opposite words *see* weak

stupid

stupid
 see opposite of clever

sturdy
 see strong

suffer
 see feel

suggest
 see say

suitable
 see good, right

supply
 see give

support
 see help

suppose
 see think

sure

swallow
 see eat

swap
 see change

sway
 see shake

swift
 see fast

sure *(adjective)*

You are **sure** if you have no doubts and know something to be right: *Jack is my oldest friend, and I am **sure** he is honest and loyal.*

certain I'm **certain** we have met before.

confident Betsy is **confident** that she'll pass her examination.

firm I was always **firm** in my belief that dogs are intelligent animals.

trusting You have such a **trusting** nature and believe what people tell you.

Same sound

shore (*noun*) It's fun to play in the tide pools along the **shore**.

Opposite words

distrustful Matt ran off with our money, and I'm **distrustful** of such people now.

doubtful It's a nice bracelet, but I think its value is **doubtful**.

uncertain He went off to Australia, and his whereabouts are **uncertain**.

124

T

take (verb)

When you **take** something, you get hold of it and possess it: *Take this book for your trip.*

bear
That bridge won't **bear** the weight of our car.

bring
Bring me a pound of apples from the market.

capture
The city has been **captured**.

carry
I'll **carry** these bags for you.

grasp
Jane **grasped** the shovel and began to dig.

seize
The federal agents **seized** the smugglers as they were carrying the barrels from their boat.

snatch
The robber **snatched** her bag.

steal
Thieves broke into the safe to **steal** gold and jewels.

Other words grab, pinch

Opposite words

give
If I win, I'll **give** you half!

reject
The editor **rejected** my poems.

see also give

125

talented
  see able, clever

talk

tap
  see hit

teach
  see show

telephone
  see call

tell
  see say, talk

tender
  see kind

terminate
  see end

terror
  see fright

test
  see try

thick
  see opposite
  of thin

talk *(verb)*

When we speak out loud and hold a conversation, we **talk**: *I'd like to **talk** to you about your vacation.*

chat   I can **chat** for hours with Tom.

discuss   I have some good ideas which I would like to **discuss** with you.

speak   Austrians and many Swiss **speak** German.

tell   **Tell** your friends that supper's ready.

speech   *(noun)* After dinner, a well-known author made a *speech*.

thin

thin *(adjective)*

If something is not very wide, or is not thick or fat, it is **thin**: *This vegetable soup is watery and **thin**.*

fine   This silk is so **fine** that you can hardly see the threads.

lean   Tom is a tall, **lean** boy, but his brother is quite plump.

narrow   That gap is too **narrow** for my car.

skinny   Bess was a **skinny** little puppy.

slender   The **slender** threads of the spider's web glittered in the sun.

sparse   This area is dry, with some **sparse** trees and bushes.

Opposite words

heavy   There was a **heavy** snowfall.

thick   **Thick** fog hid the trees from view.

dense   The woods were **dense** and overgrown.

think

thoughtful
  see nice

thoughtless
  see opposite
  of careful

throw away
  see opposite
  of keep

thrust
  see push

thump
  see hit

timid
  see quiet *and*
  opposite of bold

tiny
  see small *and*
  opposite of big

toast
  see cook

toil
  see work

think *(verb)*

If you work something out in your head, or give thought to something, you **think**: *Before I tackle any job, I like to **think** about it. I **think** I'll go to bed now.*

believe	Columbus **believed** that the world was round.
conclude	After a week with no message, we **concluded** that the ship had sunk.
consider	I **consider** this painting to be the finest of all of Picasso's work.
expect	If those clouds come near, I **expect** we'll have rain within the hour.
know	Do you **know** how the fire started?

suppose	I **suppose** the teacher is right.

touch

tough
see hard, strong

trace
see find

tranquil
see quiet

transform
see turn

transmit
see send

travel
see go

tread
see walk

tremble
see shake

trim
see cut

trip
see fall

trivial
see small

touch *(verb)*

When you put your hands on something, or feel something, you **touch** it: *It is dangerous to **touch** the live wire!* You can also be **touched** if something affects your feelings: *The teacher was very **touched** when the children presented her with a birthday gift.* Also, the word as a *noun* means "talent": *John is a great cook; he has just the right **touch**.*

affect   The whole country was **affected** by the teamsters' strike.

feel   I **feel** rather cold without my sweater.

finger   Please don't **finger** the grapes.

grope   It was so dark, I had to **grope** for the door handle.

handle   Don't **handle** that hot dish; use the potholders.

skill   (*noun*) It requires great **skill** to make clocks and watches.

see also feel

129

Transportation

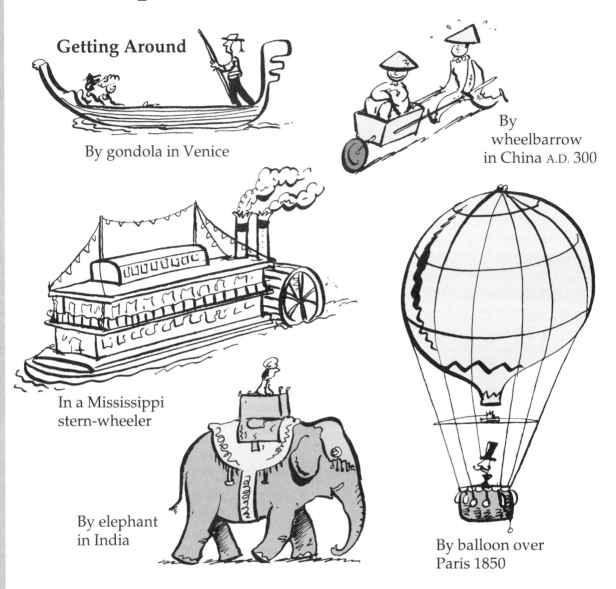

Getting Around

By gondola in Venice

By wheelbarrow in China A.D. 300

In a Mississippi stern-wheeler

By elephant in India

By balloon over Paris 1850

Car and bar

Finish off these words to find a means of getting around. The number of dashes shows the number of letters you need to make the word.

horse-drawn vehicle	car _ _ _ _ _	a small handcart	bar _ _ _
goods carried by ships	car _ _	flat-bottomed boat	bar _ _
a home on wheels	car _ _ _ _	on foot without shoes	bar _ _ _ _ _

Same vehicle, different word

American	British
streetcar	*tram*
trailer	*caravan*
airplane	*aeroplane*
subway	*underground*
bumper car	*dodgem*
engineer	*engine driver*
hood (car)	*bonnet*
gasoline	*petrol*
gear shift	*gear lever*
overpass	*flyover*
parking lot	*car park*
trunk (car)	*boot*

By air   jumbo jet

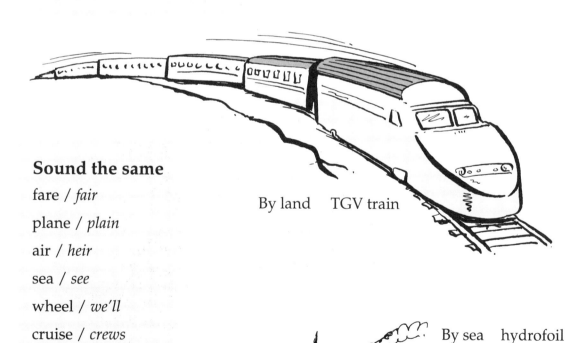

By land   TGV train

By sea   hydrofoil

Sound the same

fare / *fair*

plane / *plain*

air / *heir*

sea / *see*

wheel / *we'll*

cruise / *crews*

oar / *ore*

pedal / *peddle*

road / *rode, rowed*

trot
see run

trusting
see sure

try

try *(verb)*

When you endeavor to do something, you **try**: *I can meet you next week, but do **try** to be early.*

aim	Tim will **aim** to play better.
attempt	The water is deep, so don't **attempt** to get in unless you can swim.
strive	Sally **strives** hard at hockey, but she's not very good.
test	All the light bulbs were **tested** before being sold.
effort	*(noun)* It required some **effort** to move the large piano.

tug
see pull

tumble
see fall

turn

twist
see turn

turn *(verb)*

The word **turn** can mean several things, as in these sentences: *I shall **turn** the corner into the next street. This record player **turns** at several speeds. In autumn the leaves **turn** brown. It's my **turn** to ride the bicycle.*

change   The wizard **changed** the mice into ponies.

spin   The windmill's sails **spin** around as the wind blows.

transform   The evil spell **transformed** the prince into a frog.

twist   As Tina drew in the kite, she **twisted** the string around a stick.

wind   Make sure you **wind** the clock before going to bed.

bend   *(noun)* Be careful, there's a sharp **bend** in the road ahead.

stint   *(noun)* Fred did a six-month **stint** in the navy before moving to California.

see also change

U

ugly
see opposite of beautiful

uncertain
see opposite of sure

understand
see know, see

undo
see opposite of make

uneven
see rough

unfair
see opposite of fair

unfit
see wrong

unhappy
see sad

unimportant
see small

uninteresting
see dry

unite
see join

unkind
see mean

unoccupied
see empty

unskilled
see opposite of able

unsuitable
see wrong

unusual
see odd

upright
see right

upset
see angry, hurt

usual
see opposite of odd

utter
see say

V

vacant
see empty

vanish
see go

vary
see change

vast
see big

vibrate
see shake

visit
see call

void
see empty

W

walk

walk *(verb)*

When we move around on foot from one place to another, we **walk**: *It's such a nice day; let's* ***walk*** *home.*

go   I **go** to school every day except Saturdays and Sundays.

hike   When the summer comes, we'll **hike** in the mountains.

march   Soldiers **marched** up the hill.

step   I have something to show you. Would you **step** this way?

stride   Martha was a strong walker, and **strode** off ahead of the rest.

stroll   We **strolled** through the woods.

tread   **Tread** carefully, there may be snakes in the long grass.

see also go

Other words
strut, tiptoe, tramp

Weather and climate

Whether the weather be hot
Or whether the weather be not,
We'll weather the weather
Whatever the weather
Whether we like it or not.

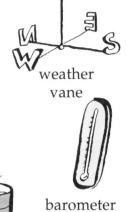
weather vane

thermometer

barometer

rain gauge

thunder and lightning

rain

downpour

drizzle

hail

sleet

precipitation

shower

raincoat

umbrella

boots

dry
drought
flood
thaw
freeze

It is cool fresh chilly cold bitter frosty
freezing icy
It is fair fine sunny mild warm heavy
muggy hot
It is damp humid dewy wet
It is misty foggy cloudy overcast murky

Sound the same

weather / *whether*

chilly / *chilli*

fair / *fare*

freeze / *frees, frieze*

hale / *hail*

mist / *missed*

rain / *reign, rein*

breeze
wind
gust
gale
squall
tempest
tornado
hurricane
cyclone
typhoon
whirlwind

137

wary
  see careful

watch
  see look, see

watchful
  see careful

water
  see wet

watery
  see weak

weak

weak *(adjective)*

Anything or anyone who is **weak** is without power or strength, and not strong: *After her illness, Jill was too **weak** to stand for long. The mooring rope was too **weak**, and the boat broke loose.*

delicate   Don't put that plate in the dishwasher; it's too **delicate**!

faint   We halted in the tunnel as we heard a **faint** sound ahead.

feeble   After being lost, our dog Rover was tired, but gave a **feeble** wag of his tail.

frail   Grandpa was quite **frail**, but happy to celebrate his birthday.

watery   You call this **watery** liquid soup?

Other words flimsy, helpless, puny

Opposite words *see* strong

wet

wet *(adjective)*

Something full of moisture, soaked in water or some other liquid, is described as **wet**: *When we were caught in the rain, our clothes got soaking **wet**.*

damp	Our shed has a leaky roof, and the inside is **damp**.
moist	There had been a heavy dew, and the ground was **moist**.
rainy	The pond is full after so many **rainy** days.
moisten	(*verb*) Sally **moistened** the flap on the envelope and sealed it.
soak	(*verb*) These beans should be **soaked** in water for two hours.
water	(*verb*) **Water** the seeds well.

see also opposite of dry

Opposite words

arid	The land was **arid**, almost as dry as a desert.
dry	Our wash has been outside for hours and is quite **dry**.
parched	We've walked for miles, and our throats are **parched**.

see also dry

wicked
  see wrong

wide
  see big

win
  see get

wind
  see turn

withdraw
  see opposite of put

withhold
  see opposite of give

work

work out
  see find

work *(noun)*

Something that needs effort to do or complete is called **work**: *It took a lot of **work**, but we have finished making our garden.*

effort   Steve had several tries and managed to jump the fence after a great **effort**.

employment   The new factory gave **employment** to many local people.

job   On Saturdays I have a regular babysitting **job**.

labor   Building the Eiffel Tower needed the **labor** of hundreds of workers.

operate   (*verb*) Our television is old, but it **operates** well.

toil   (*verb*) Coal miners **toil** each day below the ground.

Other words business, chore, occupation, profession, trade

worn
see old

worship
see love

wound
see hurt

wrong

wrong *(adjective)*

This word has two main meanings. If something is not right or correct, it is **wrong**: *Tom got all his math problems **wrong**.* Also, it means "evil": *People who do **wrong** are sent to prison. It is **wrong** to tell lies.*

false — People once thought the Earth was flat, but that is **false**.

incorrect — You have failed the spelling test because all your answers were **incorrect**.

mistaken — I thought the telephone number was 821-3452, but I was **mistaken**.

unfit — This old typewriter must be scrapped, as it's **unfit** for use.

unsuitable — The road ahead is uneven and **unsuitable** for traffic.

wicked — There have been many **wicked** people in history.

Opposite words

correct — "Pharaoh" and "siege" are the **correct** spellings.

proper — Tracey has had **proper** training in computers.

right — Is this the **right** road for St. Petersburg?

Y

yell
see call

young
see opposite of old

Same sound, different meaning

A homonym is a word that has the same sound and spelling as another but a different meaning: for example, *seal* meaning "to shut" and *seal*, the animal.
A homograph is a word with the same spelling as another but with a different meaning and sometimes a different sound: for example, *bow* meaning a ribbon and *bow* meaning to bend.
A homophone is a word with the same sound as another word, but a different spelling: for example *bear*, the animal and *bare* meaning not covered by clothes.
Here is a list of some more homophones:

adds	adz	coarse	course	idle	idol
ail	ale	cord	chord	in	inn
allowed	aloud	core	corps	its	it's
altar	alter	daze	days	knew	new
band	banned	dear	deer	knot	not
be	bee	dew	due	know	no
beat	beet	earn	urn	laze	lays
berth	birth	fair	fare	leak	leek
blew	blue	find	fined	lesson	lessen
boar	bore	fir	fur	lute	loot
boy	buoy	for	fore, four	lynx	links
brake	break	graze	grays	maid	made
buy	by	heard	herd	main	mane
cannon	canon	hear	here	meat	meet
ceiling	sealing	him	hymn	mind	mined
choose	chews	hoard	horde	muscle	mussel
clause	claws	holy	wholly	need	knead

none	nun	rack	wrack	son	sun
nose	knows	read	reed	steal	steel
ode	owed	real	reel	sweet	suite
our	hour	red	read	tail	tale
pain	pane	right	write	tease	teas, tees
past	passed	road	rowed	their	there
pause	paws	rose	rows	to	two, too
peace	piece	sail	sale	turn	tern
place	plaice	scene	seen	vain	vein
peer	pier	seam	seem	waist	waste
plain	plane	seize	seas, sees	wood	would
praise	prays, preys	slay	sleigh	yoke	yolk
prey	pray	some	sum	you	ewe

Answers

The community's helping hands (p. 25)

church	priest
synagogue	rabbi
fire station	firefighter
hospital	nurse, doctor, dentist
school	teacher
post office	mailman, mailwoman
kitchen	cook
police station	policeman, policewoman

Containers (p. 28)
Double words vessel, can, sack, sink

Family (p. 42)
Man and woman at a party: the boy is the nephew of the man's wife.

Family problems (p. 43)
grandfather (Mr. Bowles), sister (Mrs. Jones), son (John), cousin (Deri), your grandfather

Houses (p. 62)
Double words shed, flat, yard, way

Parts of a house window, door, chimney, roof/room, floor, wall, ceiling, stairs

Odd one out The Tower of Babel, because the others are still standing.

Land (p. 74)
Hidden rivers Nile, Hudson, Tigris

What animal lives where?

camel	desert
kangaroo	bush
eagle	cliff
cattle	plain
squirrel	woods
dolphin	sea

Music (p. 87)
Musical groups
strings: harp, violin, cello, guitar, double bass
woodwind: clarinet, oboe **brass**: trumpet, trombone **percussion**: xylophone, tambourine, gong

Plants (p. 98)
Fruit, flower, vegetable or tree?
fruit: pear, apple, grape, avocado, nut, pineapple, lemon **flower**: lily, tulip, iris, daffodil, daisy, nasturtium **vegetable**: lettuce, onion, carrot, bean, pea, celery, cauliflower, cassava **tree**: pear, elm, apple, beech, oak

Roots geranium, tulip, daisy, dandelion, chrysanthemum, sunflower, marigold, wallflower

Sport (p. 121)
Pairing karate, soccer, tennis, pelota, boxing, riding, skiing, runner, jumper, arrows, hockey

Divisions of sport
combat sports: boxing, fencing, judo, karate, wrestling **track and field**: high jump, long jump, pole vault, running **target sports**: archery, darts, shooting **cue sports**: billiards, pool, **winter sports**: curling, luge, skating, skiing, tobogganing **water sports**: canoeing, rowing, sailing, swimming, water polo, water-skiing **court games**: badminton, basketball, real tennis, squash, tennis **goal sports**: football, hockey, lacrosse, rugby, soccer **bat and ball games**: baseball, cricket, softball, squash, table tennis, tennis **equestrian events**: horseback riding, polo, rodeo, stadium jumping

Transportation (p. 130)
carriage, cargo, caravan, barrow, barge, barefoot